CREATING PEACE, BUILDING COMMUNITY

JUDITH BACHAY, Ph.D.

James A. Burke II, Editor
Elyse Brunt, Educational Editor
Nancy Mannion Brice, Educational Editor
Catherine H. Diekmann, Educational Editor
Graphic Design by Ron Dilley
Illustrations by Linda Bladholm
Cover Design by Tracey Flanagan

PEACE WORKS
Peace Education™
FOUNDATION

ISBN # 1-878227-42-4

HELLO BINGO

Put your first name in the center box. Next, walk around the classroom and find someone who can sign each box. Remember, a person can sign your page only once! When your page is completely filled in, let your teacher/leader know.

Find someone who...

1. Likes a movie you like
2. Plays sports
3. Has flown in an airplane
4. Has gone to a symphony
5. Listens to the same music you do
6. Sings in a choir
7. Has been in a cast
8. Has gone to summer school
9. Has gone to camp
10. Can ride a horse
11. Has a job
12. Likes to shop
14. Has the same favorite food as you
15. Likes vegetables
16. Likes the same class
17. Has visited another country
18. Was born in the same month as you
19. Belongs to a club
20. Knows how to speak two or more languages
21. Can read music
22. Has attended a family reunion
23. Wears braces
24. Reads the newspaper
25. Can surf the net

VILLAGE NOTES

Remember, your village is a place where you are safe and secure.

____

My Village's Name

Here are some examples of things that we do in our villages. As you think of other examples, add them to the list at the bottom of the page.

✦ ____________________	✦ ____________________
✦ ____________________	✦ ____________________
✦ ____________________	✦ ____________________
✦ ____________________	✦ ____________________

Rules for Fighting Fair

1. Identify the problem.
2. Focus on the problem.
3. Attack the problem, not the person.
4. Listen with an open mind.
5. Treat a person's feelings with respect.
6. Take responsibility for your actions.

FOULS

- Name Calling
- Blaming
- Sneering
- Not Listening
- Getting Even
- Put Downs
- Bringing up the Past
- Threats
- Pushing
- Hitting
- Bossing
- Making Excuses
- Not Taking Responsibility

I'm a Star

The Things That I Love to Do

List the 15 things that you most love to do.
Check the categories that apply to each activity.

Things I love to do	It involves emotional, spiritual or physical risk	It adds to my uniqueness	It is something other people might enjoy	It costs money to do	Might be gone from my list in five years
1.					
2.					
3.					
4.					
5.					
6.					
7.					
8.					
9.					
10.					
11.					
12.					
13.					
14.					
15.					

Adapted by permission of Warner Books, Inc. New York.
From ***Values Clarification*** by Dr. Sidney B. Simon, Dr. Leland W. Howe, and Dr. Howard Kirschenbaum.

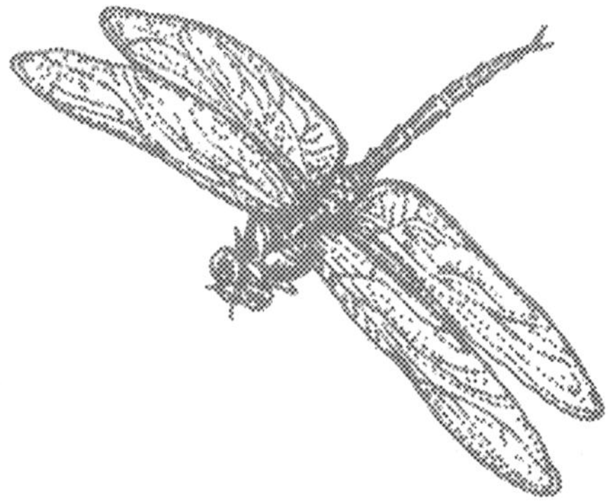

The only way to have a friend is to be one.

—Ralph Waldo Emerson

Get the Picture

The Rumor Test

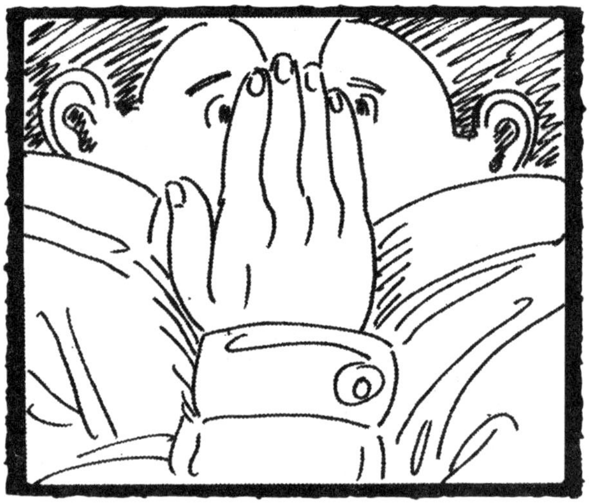

(Check the box that most accurately answers each question)

	A great deal	Some	Not much	None
1. How much of this story do you know, for a fact, to be true?				
2. How much of the information is based on someone else's account?				
3. How much trust do you have in the person who told you the story?				
4. How much distance did the information travel?				
5. How much disrespect, harm, or injustice might occur if you believe this story?				
6. How much would the person's dignity be attacked if you pass this story on?				
7. How much would it bother you to have someone tell a story like this about you?				

Listening Everywhere

We look at each other.

We focus on the speaker.

We minimize distractions.

We show respect for the other person.

We let each other have different points of view without criticizing or attacking.

We observe each other's non-verbal communication (body language, tone of voice, facial expressions)

We care about each other's feelings.

We ask questions to make sure that we understand.

We paraphrase the speaker's thoughts and feelings.

Perspective Taking

As peacemakers, we do our best to understand the other person, even if we don't totally agree with the person. To do this, it is important to find out how a person views a situation. This is called his or her *perspective*. It takes practice to develop perspective-taking skills. Here are four steps that will help you.

1. **Have a genuine interest in the speaker.**
2. **Set aside your own concerns for the moment.**
3. **Use all of your listening skills.**
4. **Imagine yourself experiencing what the speaker is telling you. Pretend you are the other person; try to imagine why the person feels the way he or she does.**

Let's practice perspective taking. Read the following scenario and complete the chart below.

Pat and Jamie were best friends in sixth grade. Over the summer, Jamie becomes friends with some older students who are popular at the junior high. Jamie starts to hang out with them. They don't want to hang out with Pat. Pat and Jamie rarely see each other anymore. At separate times, they come to talk to Chris about it. Write their responses in the chart.

Jamie's Perspective	Pat's Perspective
What is Jamie's main concern?	What is Pat's main concern?
How does that concern make Jamie feel?	How does that concern make Pat feel?

Emotions: The Keys to Developing Empathy

These are the keys that will help you to unlock the door to understanding, see the world through other people's eyes, and increase your peacemaking skills:

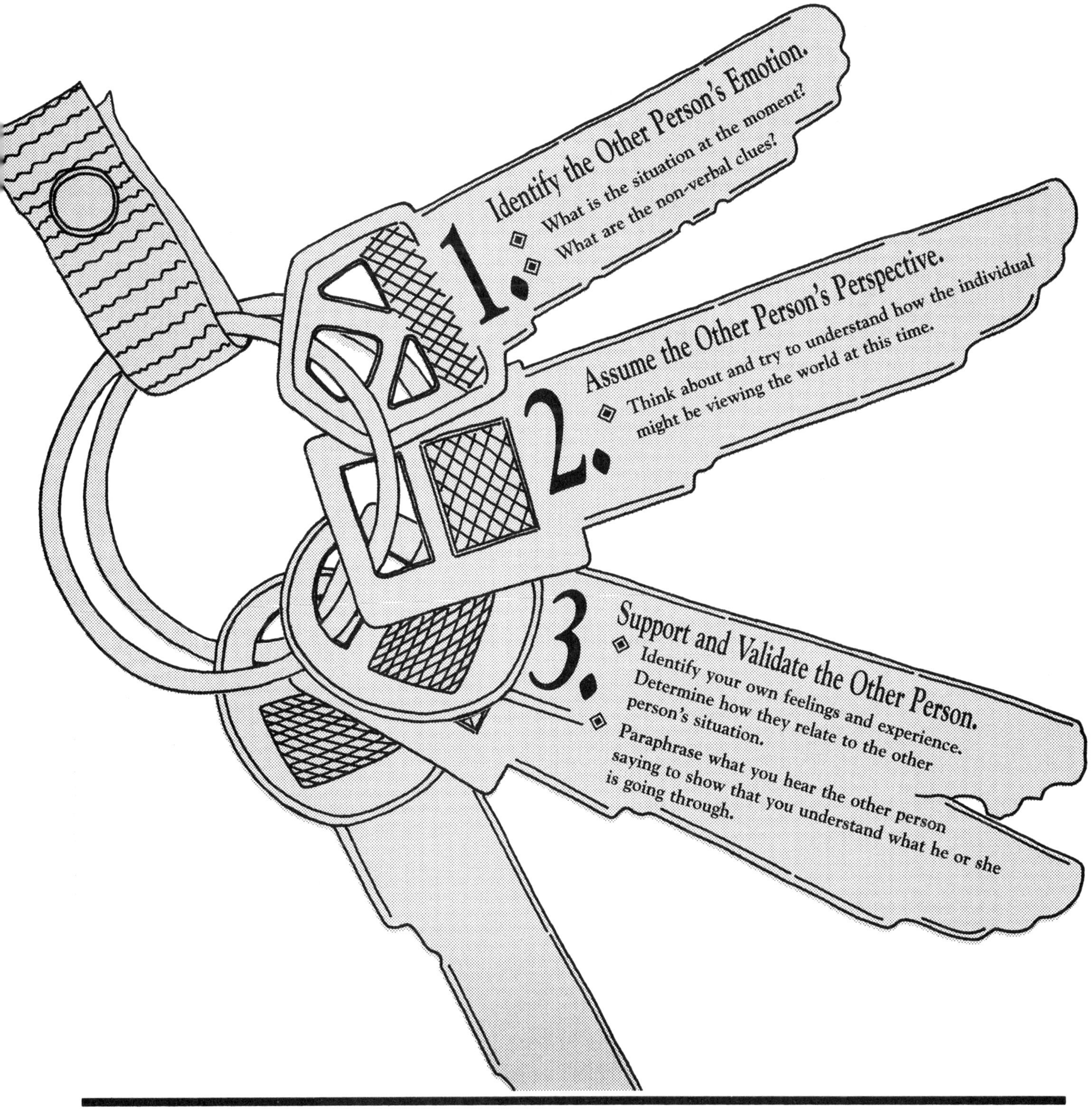

Using the I-Statement

Get Up, Stand Up, Speak Up FOR YOUR RIGHTS

Everyone has the right to be treated with respect. If your dignity is violated, you must be willing to stand up for yourself. This means we sometimes have to refuse to do things that friends may ask us to do. It's not always easy, but if you've learned the skills to stand up for yourself — in a peaceful and nonviolent manner — it is always possible.

One of the best ways to stand up for yourself is the I-Statement. The I-Statement is a response that helps you express your feelings and needs without being disrespectful to the other person.

THE I-STATEMENT:

"(The other person's name),

I feel (what the effects on your feelings are)

when you (describe the other person's behavior)

and I would like you to (what you would like the other person to do)."

CREATE YOUR OWN I-STATEMENT!

"______________________________

I feel ______________________________

when you ______________________________

and I would like you to ______________________________."

The I-Statement is an example of assertive language. Assertive language allows you to stand up for yourself in a powerful way. It increases your self-respect and self-control. Unfortunately, people often use non-productive methods of communication called aggressive language and non-assertive language.

Aggressive language is expressing your thoughts, feelings and beliefs in a way that violates the dignity of another person. When we use aggressive language we're not following the Rules for Fighting Fair. Aggressive language is a verbal form of violence.

Non-assertive language is expressing yourself in a way that does not express your thoughts, feelings, beliefs or personal needs. When you use non-assertive language, you don't stand up for yourself and end up violating your own dignity. You let others run over you.

Are you getting confused? If so, here is an example that might help to clear things up. Roberto is trying to ask his father something, but his little brother Juan keeps interrupting. Let's see what Roberto's response sounds like when he uses each style.

Get Up, Stand Up,

ASSERTIVE (I-STATEMENT):

AGGRESSIVE:

NON-ASSERTIVE:

Look at the examples on the left. Answer the following questions.

❶ What Rules for Fighting Fair were violated in the aggressive example?

❷ If Roberto's little brother feels that Roberto has attacked his personal dignity, what do you think he might say to defend himself?

❸ Other than what he says, what else might he do?

❹ Will aggressive language generally escalate or de-escalate the conflict? Why? How?

Speak Up FOR YOUR RIGHTS

In your villages, use the following examples to role play an assertive I-statement, aggressive, and non-assertive response. Observe the body language and the words so that you can demonstrate and discuss the complete communication with the class.

◈ Walking home from school, Sam lights up a cigarette. He offers one to his friend Raoul.

◈ Patrick borrows Andrew's favorite tape. When Patrick returns it, Andrew discovers that it's broken.

◈ John and Maria were best friends. John was trying to copy from Maria's test. She covered her paper. After class, Maria talked to John.

◈ Linda excitedly told her best friend Laura that she had gotten an "A" on the science test. Laura said that she had received a "F." Linda was upset because Laura ignored her for the rest of the day.

Personal Power Puzzle

Peacemakers use assertive communication to get their needs met while still showing respect for other people. Your mission is to identify statements that are assertive, aggressive, or non-assertive through color.

Directions:

Identify what kind of language each sentence uses. Match the number of each sentence with the numbers in the puzzle, then color each piece the appropriate color.

All statements that are aggressive: ....Red
All statements that are assertive: ....Green
All statements that are non-assertive:.......Yellow

When you've finished, turn the page upside down to get your message.

1. Well, I guess you can cheat off of my test, but try to be careful, O.K.?
2. I guess if everyone else is going to skip class, I will, too.
3. Don't talk to me like that, you idiot!
4. This jacket is sort of tight, but, well, I guess I can squeeze into it — I'll take it.
5. I would like my money back for this jacket.
6. Look, I told you I don't want to buy anything — are you stupid, or what?
7. Get those cigarettes out of my face before I knock you out!
8. I'm not interested in buying anything now.
9. I think you have my basketball, well, maybe not — oh, I'll just buy a new one.
10. You'd better quit looking at my test, you creep.
11. You are so annoying — go away!
12. I'm glad you didn't come to my party, you loser!
13. I don't want to smoke a cigarette. Please stop asking me.
14. I did sort of want to try out for the team, but never mind. I know I won't make it.
15. Hey, fool, that's my basketball – get your hands off it!
16. Excuse me, but you picked up my basketball. I'd like it back, please.
17. I didn't order this hamburger, but that's Okay. I'll eat it.
18. I do have a test tomorrow, but I guess maybe I can go out.
19. Why would I want to skip class with a bunch of losers like you?
20. This isn't what I ordered. Please take it back.
21. Oh, O.K., I guess one cigarette won't kill me, right?
22. I don't want to skip class, but if you want to do something after school, call me.
23. I'm late, look, I really have to go... all right, I'll stay for a few more minutes.
24. Hey, I ordered chicken. What is this garbage?

PERSONAL POWER PUZZLE

DECISION-MAKING WITHIN

Have you ever had to make up your mind? Of course you have. It's not always easy to make a decision, is it? Sometimes you have a lot of choices, and each one has its good points and bad points. How can you decide?

Here's a great way to make the *best* decision. By using the Decision-making Matrix, you can look at your options, see the good points and bad points and then choose the best solution for you. If you follow the five steps below and use the matrix, you'll find that making decisions will be easier — maybe even fun! Good luck.

1. **What's the problem?**
   You've grown a few inches and your bicycle does not fit you properly anymore. When you pedal, your knees hit the handlebars. Unfortunately, your parents told you that they won't buy you a new bike.
2. **Find the facts:**
   Your bike is uncomfortable because your knees hit the handlebars when you ride.
   Your parents said they will not buy you a new bike.
   You do not have enough money to buy yourself a new bike.
3. **IWWM: In What Ways Might...**
   IWWM you be able to fix your old bike so that you can still ride it?
   IWWM you convince your parents to buy you a new bike?
   IWWM you earn enough money to buy a new bike?
4. **Brainstorm for possible solutions:**
5. **Develop your criteria:**
   What factors will you consider when making the decision?
6. **Rate your possible solutions:**
   Rate each criterion for your possible solutions from "1" (the ones you like the least) to "5" (the ones you like the most). Add them up: The solution with the highest score is the best.

Decision-making Matrix

Define the Problem:

____

____

	CRITERIA							
POSSIBLE SOLUTIONS	EASE	YOUR COST	PRACTICAL	TIME				TOTAL
1.								=
2.								=
3.								=
4.								=
5.								=

Decision-making Matrix based on Parnes, S.J. (1992) ***The Source Book for Creative Problem Solving***
Reprinted with permission from the copyright holder, The Creative Education Foundation Press, 1050 Union Road, Buffalo, NY 14224

Decision-making Within

DECISION-MAKING WITHIN

Now that you've used the Decision-making Matrix to resolve a problem, go to your village. Let's see if you and the members of your village can resolve the following problem:

1. **What's the problem?**

   A few weeks ago, you said you would help your best friend with a science project. Now it's a Saturday night and your best friend calls you for help. The project is due Monday. You have already told some other friends that you will go to a movie with them.

2. **Find the facts:**

   You promised to help your best friend with a science project.
   It's Saturday night.
   Your best friend needs your help.
   You have told some other friends that you will go to a movie with them.
   The project is due Monday.

3. **IWWM: In What Ways Might...**

   IWWM you get out of helping with the science project?
   IWWM you get out of going to the movie?
   IWWM you be able to see the movie and help with the science project?

4. **Brainstorm for possible solutions:**

5. **Develop your criteria:**

   What factors will you consider when making the decision?

6. **Rate your possible solutions:**

   Rate each criterion for your possible solutions from "1" (the ones you like the least) to "5" (the ones you like the most).

   Go to your village and use your Creative Conflict Solving Matrix to evaluate solutions for the problem.

Decision-making Matrix

Define the Problem:

____

____

POSSIBLE SOLUTIONS	CRITERIA							TOTAL
1.								**=**
2.								**=**
3.								**=**
4.								**=**
5.								**=**

Decision-making Matrix based on Parnes, S.J. (1992) ***The Source Book for Creative Problem Solving***
Reprinted with permission from the copyright holder, The Creative Education Foundation Press, 1050 Union Road, Buffalo, NY 14224

DECISION-MAKING WITHIN

It's time to use the Decision-making Matrix to resolve a problem of your own. Think of a problem you've had recently. Answer the questions below and use the matrix to resolve the problem. Good luck!

1. **What's the problem?**

2. **Find the facts:**

3. **IWWM: In What Ways Might...**

4. **Brainstorm for possible solutions:**

5. **Develop your criteria:**

6. **Rate your possible solutions:**

Decision-making Matrix

Define the Problem:

____

____

POSSIBLE SOLUTIONS	CRITERIA							TOTAL
1.								**=**
2.								**=**
3.								**=**
4.								**=**
5.								**=**

Decision-making Matrix based on Parnes, S.J. (1992) ***The Source Book for Creative Problem Solving***
Reprinted with permission from the copyright holder, The Creative Education Foundation Press, 1050 Union Road, Buffalo, NY 14224

Do The Right Thing: PEER REFUSAL TECHNIQUES

1. ASK QUESTIONS

When someone asks you to do something that doesn't sound right, don't be afraid to ask questions:

- What are we going to do?
- Who is going to be there?
- Will I be safe? Is it possible that anyone could get hurt?
- Is this illegal?

2. COME UP WITH A REASON WHY

If you don't want to do something, give the other person a quick reason why. If you're not comfortable saying the real reason, a little humor can help to break the tension.

"My parents will kill me—it's not worth it."

"No thanks. On my allowance, I can't afford to get addicted to cigarettes."

"No way—I need every one of my brain cells for math."

3. SUGGEST OTHER THINGS TO DO

When you suggest doing something else, you let your friend know that you are rejecting the action, not the friendship.

"No, I don't want to smoke a cigarette with you, but I'll shoot some hoops or go to the movies with you if you want."

4. DON'T BE AFRAID TO SAY NO

If your friend keeps pressuring you to do something that you don't want to do, don't argue, defend yourself or spend any more time discussing it. Say no and mean it.

"No, I have to take this test. I won't skip class with you."

"I'm not going to help you steal. Please don't ask me again."

5. LEAVE

If your friend decides to use drugs, or gets you involved in a dangerous situation, leave immediately. Go home, go to class, join a group of friends or talk to someone else. Let your friend know that you will be there if and when your friend decides to change his or her behavior.

In your villages, roleplay a situation in which you use peer refusal to assert yourself and do the right thing.

"He who controls others may be powerful, but he who has mastered himself is mightier still."

– Lao Tsu

WHAT'S RIGHT FOR YOU?

Situation:	Values: How might your decision affect beliefs that are important to you? (e.g., honesty, loyalty)	Relationships: How might your decision affect the relationships you have with other people?	Self-Esteem: How will your decision affect how I feel about myself?	Consequences: What will happen if you do this?	Ethics: Is this the right thing to do?
① You can't have friends over without your parents' permission. They aren't home. You want to have a friend over. Will you?					
② You just promised a neighbor you would baby-sit. Your friends want you to go to the movies with them. Will you?					
③ The person your best friend likes asks for your phone number. What do you do?					
④ You need to improve your math grade. A friend offers to help you cheat on the exam. Will you?					

THE ANGER TREE

People get angry all the time. However, the anger that people express is not always what it seems to be. Sometimes, people use anger as a cover-up, a way to avoid expressing other feelings that they don't feel comfortable with.

For example, let's suppose Linda was cleaning the house while her mom was at work. While dusting, she dropped her Mom's favorite plate, the one with the big cows painted on it, and broke it. Linda feels several emotions:

- She feels sad; she liked the plate, too, and is sorry that it is broken.
- She feels guilty; she promised her mom that she wouldn't touch it.
- She feels stupid; this is the second thing she's broken this week.
- She feels scared; her mom will probably punish her.
- She feels frustrated; she was cleaning the house as a surprise gift to her mom and ended up breaking her mom's favorite plate.

When Linda's mom gets home, she asks Linda how the plate was broken. Linda yells, "I don't want to talk about the stupid plate! If you hadn't stuck it way up on that shelf, I never would have dropped it!" Linda then ran to her room and slammed the door.

Linda didn't want to deal with her feelings of sadness, guilt and frustration, so she covered them up by using anger to express her emotions instead. In this way, anger is like a tree; you can see only the branches and leaves—you can't see the roots that are making it grow.

THE ANGER TREE

Write in the roots of the tree feelings that you think students might keep inside or hide.

Anger Management Plan

I get angry when

Cause:	**Trigger:**
	External Event:
Effect:	**Physical response that tells me I'm angry:**
	Internal thoughts that increase anger:
Action:	**Actions I take:**
Consequence:	**Consequences of my actions:**

Anger Management Options:

Mental

Physical

Anger Management

Mental options I can use at school

Physical options I can use at school

ANGER MANAGEMENT PLAN

My Top Five Options

1. ______________________________

____

____

2. ______________________________

____

____

3. ______________________________

____

____

4. ______________________________

____

____

5. ______________________________

____

____

**After I've used my Personal Anger Management Plan,
I give myself some credit with a positive reflection:**

"I feel good that I maintained my control."

"I took responsibility for my anger."

"I did not let my anger control me."

Snap To It!

Here's a great way to control your anger. All you need is a rubber band from your teacher — and little bit of imagination.

First, make a list of your triggers. Triggers are words or actions that make you mad. For example, suppose in class every morning, the guy in front of you sits down and slams the back of his desk into yours. It drives you crazy! List some of your triggers in the box at the right:

My Triggers

Next, list the negative thoughts that occur when your anger is triggered. These negative thoughts are the first thing that pop into your mind. For example, "This guy is such a jerk! The next time he does that, I'm going to smack him in the back of the head!"

Negative Thoughts

Now, make a list of positive thoughts that can help you manage your anger effectively. For example, "I refuse to use violence. I'll count to ten to calm down. I'll tell him how much that bothers me and ask him to stop it." Write some positive thoughts in the box at the right:

Positive Thoughts

Here comes the fun part. You can stop negative thoughts by putting the rubber band around your wrist. Here's how. Look at your list of triggers. Think of each one. When you start to get angry, snap the rubber band and *mentally* scream "Stop!" as loud as you can. After you've snapped the rubber band, think of some of your positive thoughts. It sounds kind of silly, but it really works!

Keep the rubber band around your wrist so you can use it the next time someone triggers your anger. Become a capable, competent and confident problem solver. Remember:

S top the thoughts that trigger your anger.
N otice that you are in control.
A ctivate your anger management plan to work.
P at yourself on the back for becoming more capable, competent, confident — and in control.

Violence is:

Non-violence is:

By the end of eighth grade, it's likely that you will have witnessed at least 8,000 murders—on television alone! Does this mean that every eighth grader will become a murderer? Of course not. However, research has shown us that, on certain people, media violence can have negative effects:

1. **The Aggression Effect** occurs when the violence a person sees, hears or reads about in the media results in aggressive behavior, even violence, towards others.
2. **The Victim Effect** occurs when people become afraid and distrusting because they think they might become victims of the violent acts they see in the media.
3. **The Bystander Effect** occurs when people have been exposed to so much violence by the media that it doesn't bother them anymore. When this happens, people may also begin to ignore the real-life violence that they see.
4. **The Increased Appetite Effect** is exactly what it sounds like—the more violence someone sees, the more he or she wants to see.

Thankfully, there is a flip side to this coin. Media that stress caring and peacemaking skills can have positive effects on behavior:

1. **The Pro-Social Effect** occurs when a person increases helpful and caring behaviors after watching, reading or listening to materials that promote such behavior.
2. **The Aggression Reduction Effect** occurs when a person becomes less aggressive and hurtful, and practices conflict resolution after being exposed to positive examples in the media.

Violence: Name it, Count it

Using this chart, keep track of all the examples of violence and non-violence you see in the listed categories. At the end of the week, count up the incidents and write the total in the column at the right.

Category	Violent							Total
	Mon.	Tue.	Wed.	Thu.	Fri.	Sat.	Sun.	
Songs								
Movies								
School/Real Event								
Television								
Video Games								
News (T.V./Paper)								
Sports								
Internet								

Category	Non-violent							Total
	Mon.	Tue.	Wed.	Thu.	Fri.	Sat.	Sun.	
Songs								
Movies								
School/Real Event								
Television								
Video Games								
News (T.V./Paper)								
Sports								
Internet								

Conflict is a state of disagreement that occurs within or between people. While we usually think of conflict as a bad thing, the presence of conflict can be helpful. Conflict is usually a signal that something needs to change. If we use a constructive approach to resolving conflict, we can create positive change, grow as individuals and strengthen relationships.

There are several types of conflict. Conflict that occurs within a person is called **intrapersonal** conflict. This happens when a person's feelings, beliefs and ideas conflict with each other. Conflict between two or more people is called **interpersonal** conflict. Conflict occurs in **systems** too. If you watch the news, you know that there is conflict between groups, organizations and nations.

All conflicts have three elements that have to be dealt with to resolve the conflict. The **issue** includes the things that caused the conflict and need to change. The **relationship** is the association or connection between disputants. Their relationship can affect how they perceive the conflict. The **emotion** is how disputants feel. This is often related to the issue, but not the same.

It may be helpful to think of a conflict as the triangle that signals the need for change. On each end of the triangle is an element which needs to be considered and addressed:

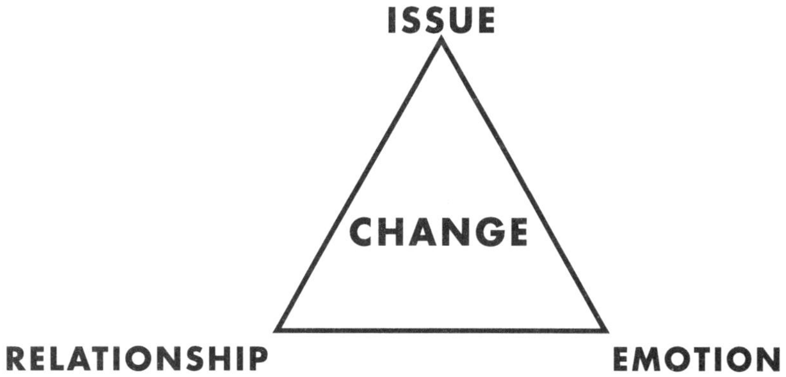

As humans, we are responsible for choices and decisions that lead to actions, and the results of those actions. Unfortunately, we are not born with the knowledge to solve conflicts. Because of this, we may develop habits that are not helpful. Analyzing the elements of a conflict and using the Rules for Fighting Fair are powerful tools for resolving conflict in a healthy, helpful manner.

CONFLICT STYLES

CONGRATULATIONS !

You now are the newest employee of Cartoons, Inc. Your first assignment is a cartoon that features all of the characters pictured below. They are all involved in a conflict with each other.
Your job: Develop the personality of each character. How do these animals usually act? What might they say to each other? How will they handle the conflict?

Sammy the Shark

Oliver the Ostrich

Felicia the Fox

Shirley the Sheep

Osborne the Owl

Now, take a look at the quotes in the box. Which of the characters would most likely say each one?

A. *"Anything you want to do is okay with me."*

B. *"It's my way or no way."*

C. *"Meet me half way."*

D. *"There's nothing I can do."*

E. *"We can make it work."*

Sammy the Shark _____ **Oliver the Ostrich** _____ **Felicia the Fox** _____

Shirley the Sheep _____ **Osborne the Owl** _____

Conflict Questionnaire

Pick one of the scenarios from the last activity. Look the list of behaviors below. In the box beside each behavior, check whether you think it would have escalated or de-escalated the conflict. In the next box, explain why.

	Escalate	De-escalate	Why?
1. Refuse to talk to the other person			
2. Tell the other person you'll hit him or her			
3. Demand the problem be resolved at once			
4. Get friends to "gang up" on the person			
5. Avoid the conflict by changing the subject			
6. See if the other person wants to resolve the problem			
7. Agree to talk at a later date to "chill out"			
8. Using your skills to understand the other person's point of view			
9. Talk behind the other person's back			
10. Agree with whatever the other person says			
11. Decide by having someone "judge" who is right			
12. Cause a scene until the person gives in			
13. Spread rumors about the other person			
14. Try to avoid the person			
15. Use verbal Fouls, like name-calling			
16. Work together to come to a compromise			
17. Tell the other person you are sorry			
18. Tell an adult what the other person did			
19. Don't let the person know how you feel			
20. Tell the other person how you feel, without blaming him or her			
21. Joke about the conflict			
22. Use physical Fouls, like hitting			
23. Use the Rules for Fighting Fair			

An adaptation of work developed by Elizabeth Loescher at The Conflict Center
2626 Osceola Street, Denver, CO 80212. (303) 433-4983

PUTTING IT

It takes a lot of different skills to productively resolve a conflict. Use the following process to put all the skills together and live up to the Rules for Fighting Fair when conflict occurs.

1. Check your emotions:

Are you angry or experiencing another intense emotion? It's hard to think clearly and take positive action when you're flooded with emotions.

Use your anger management plan or another peaceful tactic to calm down and focus.

2. Analyze the conflict:

Ask yourself: "What do I want to change?"

Identify the elements of the conflict by asking yourself:

What is/are my issue(s)?
What is my relationship with the other person?
How does the conflict make me feel?

3. Communicate with the other person:

Each person gets a chance to explain his/her perspective of the conflict without being interrupted. (Use information gathered from Step II here.)

The speaker may want to use an I-Statement to express his or her viewpoint.

The listener should use the Steps to Effective Listening (Remember to paraphrase what the speaker said to make sure that you understand correctly)

Switch roles so that everyone gets an opportunity to speak and listen.

If necessary, ask each other questions to clarify and help promote understanding.

All Together

4. **Identify the problem:**

   State clearly what you think the problem is. What needs to change?

   The problem may concern the issue, relationship, emotion or a combination of these.

   Any conflict may have more than one problem. That's okay. Deal with each problem individually. Start with the problem that's easiest to deal with.

5. **Search for solutions:**

   Focus on the problem. Brainstorm all of the possible ideas to resolve it. (If the conflict is complicated, you may want to write down all of the ideas so you don't forget any of them.)

   This is not the time to solve the conflict, so don't judge or evaluate the options yet; anything goes at this point!

6. **Choose the solution:**

   Now is the time to evaluate which idea or ideas will best resolve the conflict.

   You may want to create some criteria for judging what will work and what won't. (Remember the Decision-making Matrix. You don't have to use it; just think of some categories to evaluate the strengths and weakness of each solution)

   Decide which solution or solutions work best for both of you. Make sure you agree on what has to happen and who has to do what, and when, so that the conflict stays resolved.

   Have all of the problems been resolved? If so, proceed to step 7. If not, repeat steps 5 and 6 to resolve the remaining problems.

7. **Closing:**

   Briefly discuss what you think you could do differently in the future to prevent this from happening again.

   Give each other some credit for taking the time and effort to work through the conflict productively and respectfully.

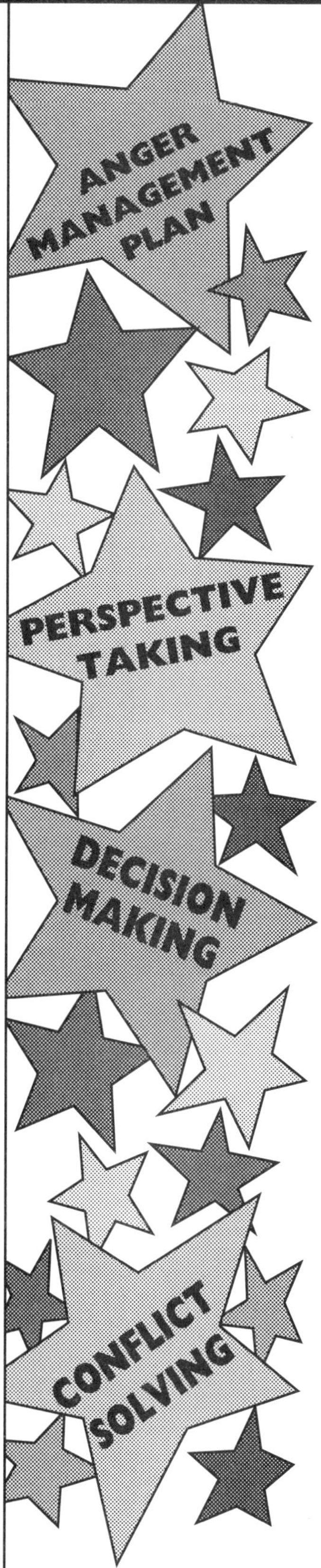

MEDIATION
MAKING PEACE, CREATING SOLUTIONS

You Can Handle It

Conflict is a normal part of life. By using the Rules for Fighting Fair, you can successfully resolve most of your conflicts. Sometimes, though, you'll find that you are just too angry or upset to resolve your conflict.

When this happens, it is good to have a neutral third party — someone who is not involved in the conflict — to help you resolve the conflict. This person is called a *mediator*.

The mediator's job is to guide the disputants through the conflict by using the Rules for Fighting Fair and the problem solving process.

Mediators have to have many skills. They need to be good listeners. To show that they're good listeners, they have to restate each disputant's perspective using their own words. This is called *paraphrasing*.

Mediators have to maintain *confidentiality*. This means they don't discuss the case with anyone except the program advisor. Mediators must be *neutral*. This means they can't take sides or look for blame.

Mediation is a process that allows people to find win/win solutions to their conflicts. The best part of mediation is that no one loses. Mediators don't take sides or choose a winner. Instead, they help people to come up with their own solution to their conflict.

Mediation

Mediators should decide who will take which section

I. Introduction:

"Thank you for coming. My name is _______________ and this is _______ ______. We are your mediators. We are not here to punish you or tell you what to do. We don't take sides and we are not judges. We are here to help you solve your own conflict peacefully.

"Everything you say here is confidential, except if it involves drugs, weapons or abuse. Does this conflict involve any of those things? If not, we can proceed. If it does, I'll have to stop the mediation and inform our advisor.

"Before we can begin, these are the rules you must agree upon:

1. **Agree to solve the conflict.**
2. **Be honest.**
3. **Listen without interrupting.**
4. **Show respect; no name-calling or put-downs.**
5. **Carry out your agreement.**

"Do you agree to the rules?" (If both disputants agree, proceed. If one or both of the disputants won't agree, stop the mediation and thank them for trying. Tell them that you will be informing your advisor of the situation.)

II. Let each person tell his or her side of the story:

"Who would like to begin?"

(To Disputant #1) **"Tell us what happened."** (Mediator paraphrases.) **"How do you feel and what caused you to feel that way?"** (Mediator paraphrases)

(To Disputant #2) **"Tell us what happened."** (Mediator paraphrases.) **"How do you feel and what caused you to feel this way?"** (Mediator paraphrases.)

Procedure

III. State the problem(s):

(The problem(s) may concern the issue, relationship, emotion or a combination of these)

"The problem(s) is/are ________________. Did I get that right?"

IV. Search for solutions:

"You both listened to each other's side of the story. What can each of you do to solve this problem? We'll write down your ideas. Then you can pick which ones you think will work best."

(Have disputants brainstorm for ideas. This is *not* the time to choose the solutions.)

V. Choose the solution:

"Which idea or ideas do you think will best solve this conflict?" (Be sure that each disputant agrees to do something.)

"Is this conflict solved?" (If so, proceed. If not, return to Step III and try again.)

(If need be, have the disputants write the solutions.)

VI. In the future:

"What do you think you could do differently to prevent this from happening again?"

VII. Closing:

"Congratulations for solving your conflict. To prevent rumors from spreading, please tell your friends that the conflict has been solved. Have a great day."

MEDIATION REVIEW

1. What are the five ground rules for mediation?

2. What did the mediators do to help disputants follow the ground rules?

3. Were the mediators listening? How could you tell?

4. What did the mediators do to identify the problem?

5. How did the disputants feel at different stages of the mediation?

6. Were there win/win solutions? What were they?

7. Did the mediators show empathy and caring? How could you tell?

8. Did the mediators show respect? How could you tell?

9. How did the mediators show that they heard what the disputants said?

10. How did the mediators keep the disputants focused on the problem? If they didn't, what happened?

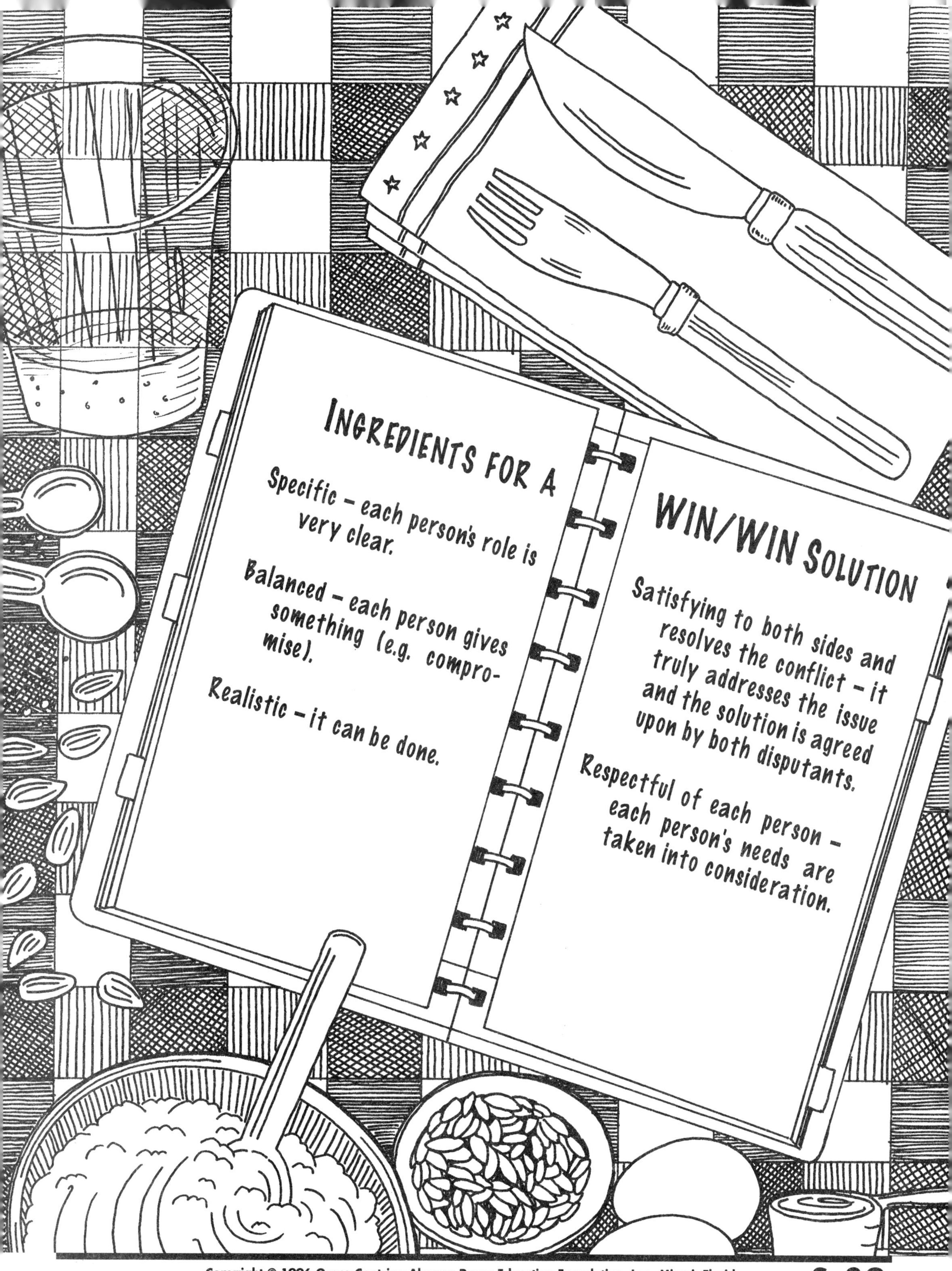
INGREDIENTS FOR A
WIN/WIN SOLUTION
Specific – each person's role is very clear.
Balanced – each person gives something (e.g. compromise).
Realistic – it can be done.
Satisfying to both sides and resolves the conflict – it truly addresses the issue and the solution is agreed upon by both disputants.
Respectful of each person – each person's needs are taken into consideration.

First they came for the communists,
and I did not speak out —
because I was not a communist.

Then they came for the trade unionists,
and I did not speak out —
because I was not a trade unionist.

Then they came for the Jews,
and I did not speak out —
because I was not a Jew.

Then they came for me —
and there was no one left
to speak out for me.

— Martin Niemöeller
(Survivor of the Holocaust)

Bully, Victim, Bystander

In order to meet their needs, bullies feel they have to use some sort of violence, or people will ignore them or try to hurt them. Bullies use **power** and **control** to:

Push people into doing what they want
Get respect and acceptance
Feel good about themselves

In groups of three, roleplay the following scenarios. Trade parts until everyone has reported as the victim, bully, and bystander.

Situation One

Place: The locker room during physical education class

Time: The class before lunch

Bully: "Hey, give me your money, you dork!"

Victim: "Um, well, you see, I don't have any money."

Bystander: (Looks away and pretends he doesn't see.)

The Bully:
Feels ______________________________

Thinks ______________________________

What kind of body language was used? ____________________

The Victim:
Feels ______________________________

Thinks ______________________________

What kind of body language was used? ____________________

The Bystander:
Feels ______________________________

Thinks ______________________________

What kind of body language was used? ____________________

Bully, Victim, Bystander

Situation Two

Place: In front of the school

When: In the morning before class

Bully: "Hey nerd, I like that hat. Did your mommy just buy it for her little boy? And look at that, it just happens to be my favorite team. Too bad for you — it's mine now!"
(Grabs hat and throws it to the bystander)

Victim: "Okay, okay, I'm a nerd. Now can I please have my hat back?"

Bystander: (Laughs. Throws the hat back to the bully)

The Bully:

Feels ______________________________

Thinks ______________________________

What kind of body language was used? ____________________

The Victim:

Feels ______________________________

Thinks ______________________________

What kind of body language was used? ____________________

The Bystander:

Feels ______________________________

Thinks ______________________________

What kind of body language was used? ____________________

Bully, Victim, Bystander

Situation Three

Place: School hallway

Time: During change of classes

Victim: (Accidentally bumps into Bully) "Oops, I'm sorry. I didn't see you."

Bully: "You did so see me, you liar! You bumped into me on purpose!" (Grabs Victim as if to hit)

Bystander: (To Bully) "Hey, chill out, girl. It was an accident." (To Victim) "Come on, we're late for class. Let's go."

The Victim:

Feels ______________________________

Thinks ______________________________

What kind of body language was used? ______________________________

The Bully:

Thinks ______________________________

Feel ______________________________

What kind of body language was used? ______________________________

The Bystander:

Feels ______________________________

Thinks ______________________________

What kind of body language was used? ______________________________

What feelings do the bully, the victim and the bystander have in common? ______________________________

____

How do the bystanders feel if they do or say nothing? ______________________________

____

As peacemakers, how can you change these situations so that they are dealt with in a nonviolent way?

____

____

Holding Up the Sky

*One day, many years ago, an elephant
saw a hummingbird lying on its back
with its little feet pointed toward the sky.*

*"Hey, Hummingbird," the elephant asked,
"what are you doing down there?"*

*"I heard that the sky will fall today,"
the hummingbird said,
"and if that really happens,
I'm going to do my part to hold it up."*

*The elephant trumpeted with laughter,
"How do you expect **THOSE** feet to hold up the **SKY**?"*

*"They can't by themselves," said Hummingbird,
"but we all must do our part,
and this is what I can do."*

— A Tale From China

What Is a Peacemaker?

A peacemaker is a person who cares about all living things and tries to understand other people's perspectives. Peacemakers are not afraid to accept and express feelings and respect themselves and others. Peacemakers work out conflicts nonviolently and take responsibility for their own actions.

Who can be a peacemaker?

Everyone can be a peacemaker. You can be a peacemaker, too, if you choose to care about yourself and the world around you. You can be a peacemaker when you believe that you can make a difference.

Who are the Peace Heroes in your life? What positive changes have these peacemakers made possible? How did they make life better for mankind? How can you honor them?

Research a courageous peace hero of your choice and find out:

Who the person is

What the person did and believed in

Where the person lived and made a difference

When the person made a difference

What motivated the person to take action

How the person put his or her beliefs into action

Peace Heroes

SUGGESTED, BUT NOT LIMITED TO:

Jane Addams
Susan B. Anthony
Corazon Aquino
John Audubon
Joan Baez
Emily Greene Balch
Leonard Bernstein
Louis Braille
Willie Brandt
Ralph Bunche
Rachel Carson
Jimmy Carter
Pablo Casals
René Cassin
Cesar Chavez
Mairead Corrigan
Norman Cousins
Jacques Cousteau
Dorthea Dix
Danilo Dolci
Amelia Earhart
Albert Einstein
Adolfo Pérez Esquivel
Galileo
Mohandas Gandhi
Mikhail Gorbachev
Dag Hammarskjöld
Thich Nhat Hanh
Audrey Hepburn
Julia Ward Howe
Thomas Jefferson
Chief Joseph
Danny Kaye
Helen Keller
Martin Luther King, Jr.
Aung San Suu Kyi
Emma Lazarus
Richard Leakey
John Lennon
Trygve Lie
Abraham Lincoln
Albert Lutuli
Horace Mann
A. J. Muste
Ralph Nader
Alfred Nobel
Robert Oppenheimer
Rosa Parks
Alice Paul
Linus Pauling
William Penn
Pablo Picasso
Diego Rivera
Eleanor Roosevelt
Sacajawea
Anwar Sadat
Carl Sagan
Andre Sakharov
Oscar Arias Sanchez
Eisaku Sato
Oscar Schindler
Albert Schweitzer
Upton Sinclair
Samantha Smith
Chief Seattle
Socrates
Elizabeth Cady Stanton
Harriet Beecher Stowe
Mother Teresa
Henry David Thoreau
Leo Tolstoi
Harriet Tubman
Bishop Desmond Tutu
Liv Ullman
Lech Walesa
Raul Wallenberg
Elie Weisel
Simon Wiesenthal
Betty Williams
Woodrow Wilson

Sacajawea

Dr. Martin Luther King, Jr.

Susan B. Anthony

PEACEMAKER'S VOCABULARY

I WALK THE TALK

PEACE WORDS	DEFINITION	WHY IT IS A PEACE WORD

Peacemaker's Vocabulary

I Walk The Talk

Words	Times said	Times acted on	Examples

What I learned about the power of words:

I Am Only One Person

I am only one person
What can one person do?

One woman
Said one word
And the buses were
Desegregated.

Rosa Parks
Was just one person.
She said one word.
She said it on December 1, 1955.

I am only one person.
What can one person do?

One person
Said
One word.
She said it on a bus.
She said it to the bus driver.
On the Cleveland Street Bus
In Montgomery.

They put her in jail,
Because she didn't "know her place,"
Because she didn't "stay in her place,"
Because she was an "uppity...."

The bus driver said,
"Stand up, ...woman,
And give up your seat
To that white man!"

It was a Thursday
When she said
That One Word,

Rosa Parks,
One person
Said one word.
The word was "No!"

On Monday morning
The buses ran.
The Negroes walked,
Each white man had two seats.
Empty seats.
Symbols of a people,
Moved to walk,
Moved to march
Moved to act
By the sound of
One woman's
One word,
"No!"

One woman
Said one word
And a nation
Blushed!

One woman
Said one word
And a world talked!

One woman
Said one word
And a nation
Blushed!

One woman
Said one word
And the Supreme Court
Acted!

— Author unknown

The Power of One

What can one person do?

Plenty!

Children all over the world have one thing in common.

They believe!

They believe that change, no matter how big the problem is, can happen.

They believe that they have the power to make change happen.

The first step to make change is to develop a plan.

Here are six steps to help you develop a plan:

1. The goal—what do you want to change?
2. What steps are you going to take? What exactly are you going to do? Be specific!
3. What resources do you need? Who can help? What information do you need?
4. What is your timeline?
5. Evaluate — did it work?
6. Reward yourself for accomplishing your goal, and making progress toward it.

In your villages, help your classmates develop individual goals. **Help** each other see yourselves as change agents. **Imagine** the steps you would take and how you would evaluate the results.

How Can I Help?

We all have our own ways of doing things. Some kinds of activities suit our personalities better than others. Here's a short quiz that will help you determine how you can best contribute.

For each question below, choose the activity that is more appealing to you and put a check in the box next to it.

After you have finished making your selections, add your scores. Give yourself two points for each check.

SECTION I

	WOULD YOU PREFER TO...		
1.	Do research about animal rights organizations		
	OR		
	Care for animals in an animal shelter?		
2.	Write a flier about protecting endangered species		
	OR		
	Distribute the flier to houses in a neighborhood?		
3.	Investigate sources of pollution in your community		
	OR		
	Participate in a community clean-up?		
4.	Brainstorm ideas to raise money for homeless families		
	OR		
	Raise money for homeless families by joining a walkathon?		
5.	Lead a class discussion about preventing school violence		
	OR		
	Patrol the school to prevent violent incidents?		
6.	Plan a project to raise money to repair a house for a low-income family		
	OR		
	Help paint a house for a low-income family?		
	TOTAL:	T:___	D:___

Understanding Your Score:

Section I: If you had more points in the "T" column, you are more of a thinker. You prefer planning, researching, and writing to physical activity. You might be good at writing newsletters, designing flyers, debating, or doing research. If you had more points in the "D" column, you are more of a doer. You might enjoy physical labor like setting up for an event, building something or handing out leaflets.

Based on ***"Changing Our World,"*** Copyright 1993, Zephyr Press, PO Box 66006, Tucson, AZ 85728

How Can I Help?

SECTION II

WOULD YOU PREFER TO...		A	T
1.	Make phone calls about saving the rain forest		
	OR		
	Go to a large "Save the Rain forest" rally?		
2.	Read and study about other cultures		
	OR		
	Join an intercultural understanding study group?		
3.	Write articles for a human rights newsletter		
	OR		
	Act as a "big brother" or "big sister" to one child?		
4.	Write letters to your senator about prison reform		
	OR		
	Visit your senator with a group to discuss prison reform?		
5.	Make tapes of books for a blind person		
	OR		
	Read to a blind person?		
6.	Think about the dangers of nuclear war		
	OR		
	Talk with your friends about the dangers of nuclear war?		
	TOTAL:	A:___	T:___

Understanding Your Score:

Section II: If you had more points in the "A" column, you prefer to work alone. You might be good at letter-writing and telephoning. If you had more points in the "T" column, you like to be part of a team. You might enjoy working on a committee, attending a rally or participating in a march.

Based on ***"Changing Our World,"*** Copyright 1993, Zephyr Press, PO Box 66006, Tucson, AZ 85728

How Can I Help?

SECTION III

WOULD YOU PREFER TO...			
1.	Give a speech about your favorite cause		
	OR		
◆	Listen to a speech about your favorite cause?		
2.	Chair a committee meeting		
	OR		
◆	Take notes at a committee meeting?		
3.	Make the arrangements for a fund-raising dance		
	OR		
◆	Sell tickets to the dance?		
4.	Organize a neighborhood watch in your community		
	OR		
◆	Be a member of a neighborhood watch in your community?		
5.	Organize a tutoring program for young students		
	OR		
◆	Work as a tutor for young students?		
6.	Direct a play that teaches children about good nutrition		
	OR		
◆	**Take or** play a role in a skit that teaches about good nutrition?		
	TOTAL:	L: ___	S: ___

Understanding Your Score:

Section III: If you had more points in the "L" column, you are a leader. You like speaking for the group and making sure that things get done. You might make a good spokesperson or chairperson of an event. If you scored higher in the "S" column, you prefer serving as a supporter. You might enjoy behind-the-scenes work like stuffing envelopes, keeping records or answering questions.

Based on ***"Changing Our World,"*** Copyright 1993, Zephyr Press, PO Box 66006, Tucson, AZ 85728

We Can Change the World – Step by Step Day by Day

"Enough committed fleas can make even the largest dog move."
— Marion Wright Edelman

Kids who care can make a difference. After deciding upon an issue that concerns you, follow these 10 Steps for Successful Service Projects to create a fun, meaningful and valuable project.

1. Research your project.
   How can you help?
2. Organize your group.
   Think about including people of all ages.
3. Find a sponsor.
   Ask an adult to work with you.
4. Make a plan.
5. Think about the needs of the recipients.
6. Decide where you are going to perform your service.
7. Get any permissions you need to take action.
8. Let other people know the good news about your project.
9. Fund raise if you need equipment or supplies.
10. Evaluate what you accomplished.

What can we accomplish as a classroom community to make our world a more peaceful place?

Find Out the Facts

You can contact these organizations to find out the facts about possible service projects.

World hunger

World Hunger Education Service
PO BOX 29056
Washington D.C. 20017
(202) 298-9503

How to hold an athletics contest for people with special needs

Special Olympics International
1350 New York Avenue NW, Suite 500
Washington, D.C. 20005
(202) 628-3630

Helping older people

National Council for Senior Citizens
1331 F Street, NW
Washington, D.C. 20004
(202) 347-8800

How to organize a concert to benefit your cause

Shoemaker, Joanie. *Note By Note: A Guide to Concert Production*
Redwood Cultural Work
Community Music & Friends
P.O. Box 10408
Oakland, CA 94608

How to make a law, change a law

Activism 2000 Project
PO Box E
Kensington, MD
20895